Travel Journal
Punta Cana

VPJournals

Copyright © 2015 VPJournals

All rights reserved.

ISBN-13: 978-1518845697
ISBN-10: 151884569X

Contact Details

Name:

Email address:

Tel:

Address:

Important Medical Information

Blood type:

Medication:

CONTENTS

Hi, I hope you enjoy this journal. It is packed with cool stuff and recommendations for you trip to Punta Cana, and has plenty of space to record details of your trip.

What's Inside	Page
Before you go to Punta Cana	
Great places to visit in Punta Cana	6-7
Cool places to visit in Punta Cana with kids	8-9
Good places to eat	10-11
Research Punta Cana	12-13
Postcard & Packing List	14-19
Punta Cana facts	21-22
Helpful hints	23-26
Clothes and shoe sizing charts, to help you get the right sizes while there	
Punta Cana Trip Diary	27-111
21 day trip diary to record details of your trip	
Reflect on you Trip	
Summary of your trip	113-121
People you met	123-125
Useful Resources	127-136
Size conversion charts	129-132
Common Translations	133-134
Notes	135-136

Have fun in Punta Cana

Great Places to visit in Punta Cana

Jesus Maestro Parish	✓
Hoyo Azu	
Bavaro Beach	
Macao Beach	
Indigenous Eyes Ecological Park	
Isla Catalina	
Laguna Bavaro	
Saona Island	
La Caiba	
Macao Beach	
Marinarium	
Playa La Vacama	

Lemon Lagoon	
Uvero Alto	
Zadanja	
Fun Fun Cave	
Seaquarium Underwater Adventure	
Parque Nacional Los Haitises	
ChocoMuseo (Chocolate Museum)	
'Natural Pool' lagoon	
Anumaya	
Dolphin Island	
Country Adventure Safari	
Los Haitises National Park	
Seaquarium Underwater Adventure	

Cool Places to visit with Kids

Sirenis Aquagames Punta Cana	✓
Manati Park Bavaro	
ChocoMuseo (Chocolate Museum)	
'Natural Pool' lagoon	
Anumaya	
Punta Cana Zipline Canopy Adventure	
Dolphin Island	
Country Adventure Safari	
Fun Fun Cave	
Los Haitises National Park	
Seaquarium Underwater Adventure	
Bavaro Beach	

Macao Beach	
Hoyo Azul	
Boat Tour	
Indigenous Eyes Ecological Park	
Rais Ranch, horse riding	
Cave Oleg Bat House	
Pirate Rum Factory & Cave Tour	
Outback Adventures Safari	
San Juan Shopping Center	
Balloon Ride	
Helicopter Tour	
Saona Island	
Isla Catalina	

Good Places to Eat in Punta Cana

Hard Rock Cafe - Punta Cana	✓
The JellyFish Restaurant	
Passion by Martin Berasategui	
Kukua Beach Club	
Captain Cook Restaurant	
Juanillo Beach, Food & Drinks	
La Palapa by Eden Roc	
Pastrata Punta Cana Restaurant	
Huracan Cafe	
La Yola Restaurant	
Nam Nam	
Playa Blanca Restaurant	
Balicana	

Le Petit Jardin	
The Beach Club	
Noah Restaurant & Lounge	
Citrus Restaurant	
Simon Mansion & Supper Club	
Soles Chill Out Bar	
The Market	
The Greek Sports Bar And Grill	
Oesterreicherhaus	
Toro	
Bamboo Restaurant	
Chez Mon Ami	
Antonio Steak House	
Mediterraneo Restaurant	
Los Gallos	

Best Websites to Research Further

Do some more research on the internet to plan your trip:

www.puntacana.com
www.punta-cana.info
www.puntacana-travelguide.com
www.puntacana.net
www.iheartdr.com/attractions/punta-cana-area
www.dominicanrepublic.com
www.domrep.org
www.godominicanrepublic.com
www.lonelyplanet.com/dominican-republic
www.wikipedia.org/wiki/Punta_Cana

More places I want to visit on our trip

1.
2.
3.
4.
5.
6.
7.
8.
9.
10.
11.
12.
13.
14.
15.

Postcard List

Name:
Address:

Name:
Address:

Name:
Address:

Name:

Address:

Name:

Address:

Name:

Address:

Name:

Address:

Name:

Address:

Name:

Address:

Name:

Address:

Name:

Address:

Name:

Address:

Name:

Address:

Name:

Address:

Packing List

✓	This Journal
	Tickets
	Passport
	Money
	Chargers
	Batteries
	Book to read
	Camera
	Tablet
	Sun glasses
	Sun cream

	Toiletries
	Water
	Watch
	Snacks
	Umbrella
	Towel
	Guide book
	Kindle
	Jacket
	Medication
	Add more below

Punta Cana Facts

- The name Punta Cana refers to the cane palms in the region, and literally means "Tip of the White Cane Palms"

- Punta Cana and Bavaro are nicknamed La Costa del Coco, or the Coconut Coast

- The currency used in Punta Cana is The Dominican peso

- Punta Cana was only developed around 45 years ago. In 1969, investor Frank Rainieri, Ted Kheel and 40 other investors bought this land and constructed the first resort, the Punta Cana Club

- The name Punta Cana was a commercial brand name for the group of investors, chosen for the fan-shaped Cana palm leafs that flourish in the area.

- The Punta Cana International Airport is one of the busiest and best connected airports in the Caribbean. It is the world's first and most successful, privately built, owned, and managed international airport

- The beaches stretch for more than 35 miles (55 km)

- Puna Cana was originally called Drunkard's Point

- The Dominican Republic's number one source of income is tourism, and Punta Cana is the country's most important tourism region

- Punta Cana has 10 beaches

- Punta Cana has become one of the premier golf destinations in the Caribbean, voted for two consecutive years in a row as the "Best Golf Destination of the Caribbean and Latin America" by the International Association of Golf Tour Operators.

- The main religion in Punta Cana is Roman Catholic

- The late Oscar de la Renta and Julio Iglesias both have homes in Punta Cana and are partners with the Grupo Punta Cana, the guys who got it all started. Oscar de La Renta is famous for designing beautiful wedding dresses and dressing first ladies, but he also designed the Tortuga Bay Boutique Hotel in Punta Cana. Mega music star Julio Iglesias has a home close to Club Med and frequently holds concerts in Punta Cana

- The coast of Punta Cana borders the Atlantic Ocean to the north; and the Caribbean Sea in the south

Clothes & Shoe Sizes

Children's Shoe Sizes

UK	EUROPE	US	Japan
4	20	4½ or 5	12 ½
4 ½	21	5 or 5½	13
5	21 or 22	5½ or 6	13 ½
5 ½	22	6	13½ or 14
6	23	6½ or 7	14 or 14½
6 ½	23 or 24	7 ½	14½ or 15
7	24	7½ or 8	15
7 ½	25	8 or 9	15 ½
8	25 or 26	8½ or 9	16
8 ½	26	9½	16 ½
9	27	9½ or 10	16 ½ or 17
10	28	10½ or 11	17 ½
10½ or 11	29	11½ or 12	18
11 ½	30	12½	18 or 18 ½
12	31	13	19 or 19 ½
12 ½	31	13 or 13½	19 ½ or 20
13	32	1	20
13 ½	32 ½	1 ½	20 ½
1	33	1½ or 2	21
2	34	2½ or 3	22

Children's Clothing Sizes

UK	EUROPE	US	Australia
12m	80cm	12-18m	12m
18m	80-86cm	18-24m	18m
24m	86-92cm	23-24m	2
2-3	92-98cm	2T	3
3-4	98-104cm	4T	4
3-5	104-110cm	5	5
5-6	110-116cm	6	6
6-7	116-122cm	6X-7	7
7-8	122-128cm	7 to 8	8
8-9	128-134cm	9 to 10	9
9-10	134-140cm	10	10
10-11	140-146cm	11	11
11-12	146-152cm	14	12

Women's Shoe Sizes

UK	EUROPE	US	Japan
3	35 ½	5	22 ½
3 ½	36	5 ½	23
4	37	6	23
4 ½	37 ½	6 ½	23 ½
5	38	7	24
5 ½	39	7 ½	24
6	39 ½	8	24 ½
6 ½	40	8 ½	25
7	41	9 ½	25 ½
7 ½	41 ½	10	26
8	42	10 ½	26 ½

Women's Clothes Sizes

UK	US	Japan	France / Spain	Germany	Punta Cana	Australia
6/8	6	7-9	36	34	40	8
10	8	9-11	38	36	42	10
12	10	11-13	40	38	44	12
14	12	13-15	42	39	46	14
16	14	15-17	44	40	48	16
18	16	17-19	46	42	50	18
20	18	19-21	48	44	52	20

Men's Shoe Sizes

UK	EUROPE	US	Japan
6	38 ½	6 ½	24 ½
6 ½	39	7	25
7	40	7 ½	25 ½
7 ½	41	8	26
8	42	8 ½	27 ½
8 ½	43	9	27 ½
9	43 ½	9 ½	28
9 ½	44	10	28 ½
10	44	10 ½	28 ½
10 ½	44 ½	11	29
11	45	12	29 ½

Men's Suit / Coat / Sweater Sizes

UK / US / Aus	EU / Japan	General
32	42	Small
34	44	Small
36	46	Small
38	48	Medium
40	50	Large
42	52	Large
44	54	Extra Large
46	56	Extra Large

Men's Pants / Trouser Sizes (Waist)

UK / US	Europe
32	81 cm
34	86 cm
36	91 cm
38	97 cm
40	102 cm
42	107 cm

We have included another copy of this at the back of the book, so you can find it quickly again when you are in Punta Cana

Punta Cana Trip Diary

Write a daily diary during your trip

Day 1

Date: _____   Weather: _____

Day 2

Date: _____   **Weather:** _____

Day 3

Date: _____   **Weather:** _____

Day 4

Date: _____   **Weather:** _____

Day 5

Tip! Send your postcards

Date: Weather:

Day 6

Date: _____   **Weather:** _____

Day 7

Date: _____   **Weather:** _____

Day 8

Date: _____ **Weather:** _____

Day 9

Date: _____ **Weather:** _____

Day 10

Date: _____   **Weather:** _____

Day 11

Date: _____   **Weather:** _____

Day 12

Date: _____   **Weather:** _____

Day 13

Date: _____   **Weather:** _____

Day 14

Date: _____   **Weather:** _____

Day 15

Date: _____   **Weather:** _____

Day 16

Date: _____   Weather: _____

Day 17

Date: _____   **Weather:** _____

Day 18

Date: _____   **Weather:** _____

Day 19

Date: _____   **Weather:** _____

Day 20

Date: _____   **Weather:** _____

Day 21

Date: _____   **Weather:** _____

Memories of your Trip

Things I will remember from the trip

Favorite Places visited on the Trip

People I Met

Name:
Address:
Tel:
email:

Name:
Address:
Tel:
email:

Name:
Address:
Tel:
email:

Name:

Address:

Tel:

email:

Name:

Address:

Tel:

email:

Name:

Address:

Tel:

email:

Name:

Address:

Tel:

email:

Name:
Address:
Tel:
email:

Name:
Address:
Tel:
email:

Name:
Address:
Tel:
email:

Name:
Address:
Tel:
email:

We hope you enjoyed your trip to Punta Cana

Please leave us a review if you found this Journal useful

Check out our useful resources on the next few pages

Clothes & Shoe Sizes

Children's Shoe Sizes

UK	EUROPE	US	Japan
4	20	4½ or 5	12 ½
4 ½	21	5 or 5½	13
5	21 or 22	5½ or 6	13 ½
5 ½	22	6	13½ or 14
6	23	6½ or 7	14 or 14½
6 ½	23 or 24	7 ½	14½ or 15
7	24	7½ or 8	15
7 ½	25	8 or 9	15 ½
8	25 or 26	8½ or 9	16
8 ½	26	9½	16 ½
9	27	9½ or 10	16 ½ or 17
10	28	10½ or 11	17 ½
10½ or 11	29	11½ or 12	18
11 ½	30	12½	18 or 18 ½
12	31	13	19 or 19 ½
12 ½	31	13 or 13½	19 ½ or 20
13	32	1	20
13 ½	32 ½	1 ½	20 ½
1	33	1½ or 2	21
2	34	2½ or 3	22

Children's Clothing Sizes

UK	EUROPE	US	Australia
12m	80cm	12-18m	12m
18m	80-86cm	18-24m	18m
24m	86-92cm	23-24m	2
2-3	92-98cm	2T	3
3-4	98-104cm	4T	4
3-5	104-110cm	5	5
5-6	110-116cm	6	6
6-7	116-122cm	6X-7	7
7-8	122-128cm	7 to 8	8
8-9	128-134cm	9 to 10	9
9-10	134-140cm	10	10
10-11	140-146cm	11	11
11-12	146-152cm	14	12

Women's Shoe Sizes

UK	EUROPE	US	Japan
3	35 ½	5	22 ½
3 ½	36	5 ½	23
4	37	6	23
4 ½	37 ½	6 ½	23 ½
5	38	7	24
5 ½	39	7 ½	24
6	39 ½	8	24 ½
6 ½	40	8 ½	25
7	41	9 ½	25 ½
7 ½	41 ½	10	26
8	42	10 ½	26 ½

Women's Clothes Sizes

UK	US	Japan	France / Spain	Germany	Punta Cana	Australia
6/8	6	7-9	36	34	40	8
10	8	9-11	38	36	42	10
12	10	11-13	40	38	44	12
14	12	13-15	42	39	46	14
16	14	15-17	44	40	48	16
18	16	17-19	46	42	50	18
20	18	19-21	48	44	52	20

Men's Shoe Sizes

UK	EUROPE	US	Japan
6	38 ½	6 ½	24 ½
6 ½	39	7	25
7	40	7 ½	25 ½
7 ½	41	8	26
8	42	8 ½	27 ½
8 ½	43	9	27 ½
9	43 ½	9 ½	28
9 ½	44	10	28 ½
10	44	10 ½	28 ½
10 ½	44 ½	11	29
11	45	12	29 ½

Men's Suit / Coat / Sweater Sizes

UK / US / Aus	EU / Japan	General
32	42	Small
34	44	Small
36	46	Small
38	48	Medium
40	50	Large
42	52	Large
44	54	Extra Large
46	56	Extra Large

Men's Pants / Trouser Sizes (Waist)

UK / US	Europe
32	81 cm
34	86 cm
36	91 cm
38	97 cm
40	102 cm
42	107 cm

Common Translations

English	French	Spanish	Italian
Hello	Bonjour	Hola	Ciao
Goodbye	Au revoir	Adiós	Arrivederci
Yes	Oui	Sí	Si
No	Non	No	No
Please	S'il-vous-plaît	Por favor	Per favore
Thank you	Merci	Gracias	Grazie
Excuse me	Excusez-moi	Perdón	Mi scusi
How much	Combien	Cuánto	Quanto
My name is	Mon nom est	Mi nombre es	Io mi chiamo
Where is	Où est	Dónde está	Dov'è
The bank	La banque	El banco	La banca
The toilet	Les toilettes	El baño	Il bagno

German	Japanese	Mandarin	Hindi
Hallo	Kon'nichiwa	Ni hao	Namaste
Auf Wiedersehen	Sayonara	Zaijian	Alavida
Ja	Hai	Shi de	Ham
Nein	Ie	Meiyou	Nahim
Bitte	Onegaishimasu	Qing	Krpaya
Vielen Dank	Arigato	Xiexie	Dhan'yavada
Entschuldigung	Sumimasen	Duoshao	Mujhe mapha karem
Wie viel	Ikura	Wo de mingzi shi	Kitana
Mein Name ist	Watashinonamaeha	Nali	Mera nama hai
Wo ist	Doko ni aru	Yinhang	Kaham hai
Die Bank	Ginko	Yinhang	Bainka
Die Toilette	Toire	Cesuo	Saucalaya

Notes:

CPSIA information can be obtained
at www.ICGtesting.com
Printed in the USA
LVOW04s0333030417
529389LV00012B/298/P